4
5

Driv

Other Books by Leigh Anne Jasheway

Bedtime Stories for Dogs

Bedtime Stories for Cats

The Rules for Dogs:
The Secret to Getting Free Treats for Life

The Rules for Cats:
The Secret to Getting Free Catnip for Life

Give Me a Break:
For Women Who Have Too Much to Do!

www.andrewsmcmeel.com

ISBN: 0-8362-3588-6

Library of Congress Catalog Card Number: 97-71379

Design and composition by Top Dog Design

Driving for Idiots

Leigh Anne Jasheway

Andrews McMeel
Publishing

Kansas City

Driving for Idiots

There are a lot of idiots out there on the road.
You know. You've exchanged insurance information with them.

Aren't you sick and tired of drivers who make
a left turn from the far right lane, come to a complete stop when entering the freeway, and leave
on their blinker through the entire state of Texas?
Wouldn't you like to show them just how annoying
they are?

Well, that's where *Driving for Idiots* comes in!

You've probably figured out by now that idiot
drivers obviously didn't learn to drive by the
same set of rules that you did. You're right! And
now you can learn their rules and become an idiot
driver yourself! If you can't beat 'em, join 'em on
the freeway.

Table of Contents

How to Get Your Idiot License

Idiot License Types

In order to receive an Idiot Driver's License, you must first prove beyond a shadow of a doubt that you are an idiot. A ticket stub from any movie featuring a former *Saturday Night Live* comic is all that is usually needed. If you do not have one of these, please bring your tenth-grade report card and a photo of yourself voting for the Martian Party in the last election.

There are three types of Idiot Driver's Licenses:

◆ **Class A Commercial license.** This license is issued to drivers who know all the words to every television commercial since the 1960s. Drivers will be tested on their ability to sing commercial jingles while either merging into oncoming traffic or dancing on the hood of their vehicles (depending upon the song).

◆ **Class B license.** Drivers whose IQs are less than one-tenth their body weight are issued this type of license, provided they can actually find the Department of Motor Vehicles for the test. Unfortunately, many drivers in this category often end up at the Department of Large Appliances at Sears instead and have to take their test on a five-speed washing machine.

◆ **Class C license.** This license is issued to any driver who fails his or her vision test. Drivers with this type of license are required to use a flashing red light and siren whenever they enter the freeway.

Each type of license may also carry provisions. These are:

◆ Must wear pacemaker

◆ Cannot drive after Labor Day

◆ Driver not allowed to use reverse

◆ No chickens allowed in vehicle except in emergencies

◆ Driver wearing shoe lifts

◆ Only with Mom's permission

Who May Apply for an Idiot License

As a general rule, any idiot may apply, but some are given special consideration. They include:

◆ Idiots with dangerous dogs

◆ Idiots in politics

◆ Idiots with diplomatic immunity

◆ Idiots who are the examiner's mother-in-law

◆ Idiots with nicknames like "The Exterminator"

◆ Idiots with ties to the Mob

◆ Idiots with no fashion sense

◆ Idiots with steel-plated boots or skulls

◆ People who play idiots on TV

◆ Pets of idiots

Idiot Driver's Exam

The Idiot Driver's Exam consists of five tests:

◆ **Vision test.** You will be asked to close your eyes and "see" whether the driver ahead of you passes his or her road test. Extra points are awarded if you can also predict the winning lottery numbers.

◆ **Knowledge test.** Idiot drivers are required to have no knowledge whatsoever. If you've recently served jury duty, you'll easily pass this test.

◆ **Road test.** You will be asked to maneuver a vehicle out of the parking lot and into traffic for fifteen minutes. Your score will be affected by the number of pedestrians who jump out of your way, the number of people who present you with the middle finger, and the number of different shades of paint you can add to your bumper by casually brushing up against other vehicles on the road.

◆ **Pee in the cup test.** Somewhere midway during the road test, usually while making a U-turn onto a one-way street, the examiner will ask you to pee in a cup. Be sure not to pee in his coffee mug.

◆ **Parking test.** Instead of being asked to parallel park, the idiot driver is asked to parallelogram park. You will be presented with four parking spaces—a trapezoid, a rhomboid, a parallelogram, and a black hole. Choose carefully and remember, no real idiot has any idea what the last sentence said.

The Idiot Driver's Role

Now that you have your Idiot Driver's License, it is important to understand the role you will play when you are out in traffic. To sum up, that role is to make other drivers' lives miserable.

Regular drivers are told never to drive while tired, drunk, angry, or under the influence of cold medication. These rules, of course, do not apply to idiot drivers. The rule for idiot drivers is:

Never drive while clinically dead (unless you have a note from home).

You may, on the other hand, drive while:

◆ Blindfolded

◆ Both feet are asleep

◆ Having a lobotomy

◆ Restrained in a straitjacket

◆ Holding your breath

◆ Having an allergic reaction to a bee sting

- Under the influence of your mother-in-law

- In a coma

- Inverted

- Invertebrate

- Insane

Idiot Vehicle Equipment

In order to be a true idiot driver, it is not enough that you have the IQ of blue-green algae and the coordination skills of, well, blue-green algae. It is also vital that your vehicle is in the right condition.

While regular drivers have to assure that their vehicles are safe and in good running condition, idiot drivers must make sure their vehicles have had all their shots, including rabies and diphtheria/tetanus. Ask your veterinarian if you're not sure.

Types of Idiot Vehicles

Idiot drivers can't just show up at a used car lot and drive off in a vehicle. You wouldn't want to get stuck with a car that makes other drivers respect and admire you (such as a BMW or Lexus). You should choose your vehicle from among the following choices:

◆ A motorcycle that belches more smoke than Detroit on a bad day

◆ A yellow cab with its horn stuck

◆ An old mail truck with Grateful Dead stickers plastered across the entire windshield

◆ A rusted out Pinto with a leaking gas tank

◆ A farm tractor so slow snails actually pass it and yell, "Outta the road, you slug!"

◆ A fifty-foot limo with no hubcaps and no brakes

◆ An RV with a bumper sticker that reads, "Yes, I Do Own the Road"

◆ A hearse painted purple and yellow

◆ A prison transport vehicle

Required Idiot Equipment

Idiot vehicles are required to have certain equipment. For your information, we have compared this equipment to that required in regular vehicles. Do not get confused. And if you do, simply shake your head from side to side and say, "What do you expect, I'm an idiot."

Regular Vehicle Equipment	Idiot Vehicle Equipment
Headlights	Head lice
Taillights	Tail feathers

Regular Vehicle Equipment	**Idiot Vehicle Equipment**
Brake lights	Brakes? What brakes?
Turn signals	An AM radio that picks up signals from alien life-forms
Parking lights	Who needs parking lights? Parking is something you should do in the dark so your date can't see that scar from when you sat on the hibachi last year.

Regular Vehicle Equipment	Idiot Vehicle Equipment
Exhaust system	Exhaust-creating system. Every idiot car must emit at least triple the government-allowed amount of pollutants. A car that also belches is a rare find.
Windows and windshield	At least one non-functioning door, preferably on driver's side. Windows are optional, but if present, should be covered with more dirt than the Sahara Desert.

Regular Vehicle Equipment	Idiot Vehicle Equipment
Rearview mirror	Velvet painting of Elvis
Horn	Horn that plays the theme song to *Dukes of Hazzard*
Fenders	Duct tape

Idiot Vehicle Cleanliness

You can usually tell a nonidiot driver by the lack of dirt in which someone has scribbled, "Wash me now!" Regular drivers think that a clean car has better fuel efficiency and resale value. An idiot driver doesn't care about these things because an idiot driver is more concerned about important things like making it to the equator before dark without taking a bathroom break.

As a general rule of thumb, an idiot driver only washes his or her car when:

- There are zucchini sprouting in the glove compartment

- An officer of the law writes out a ticket for driving under the influence of dirt

- It whimpers when you drive by a car wash

- Neighbors take up a collection of quarters for you

- There are Bee Gees concert tickets in the ashtray

- Local gang artists can't find a place to tag it

Rules of the Road

If everyone followed the same rules of the road, no one would ever experience anger, frustration, annoyance, irritability, frenzy, fury, ire, agitation, delirium, derangement, wrath, animosity, hostility. . . . And that, of course, would never work.

That's why idiot drivers have their own special rules. In order to drive like an idiot, you must forget all the regular driving rules you learned and learn the new idiot rules. If you have difficulty

remembering the new idiot rules,
simply tape them to your windshield
where you can see them every time
you get in the car.

Speed and Lane-Use Rules

You may have noticed that occasionally alongside the road there are these
white signs with black numbers on them.
These are known as "speed limits."
They are numbers that are chosen ran-
domly by engineers in between playing
computer games and giving each other
noogies.

Regular drivers, because they are obsessive, will usually only travel at the speed posted on speed limits. This just shows their complete lack of creativity. Idiot drivers, on the other hand, usually travel the speed of:

◆ Mile markers

◆ The price of a six-pack of beer

◆ The distance to the next town

◆ The exit number

◆ The sum of the numbers of the license plate of the car in front of them

◆ The frequency of the only radio station they pick up

Hydroplaning Can Be Fun

When the road is wet or your seat
is wet, different speed limit rules apply.
In these situations, you should use this
guideline:

> *Take your resting pulse
> before you get out of bed.
> Subtract your age and your
> hip size. Divide by your ex-
> spouse's income and multiply
> by the number of parking
> tickets in your glove box.*

Look Ma, No Traction!

On days when it's icy (such as
when someone just threw a Big Gulp
on the road), there is a special speed

limit rule. You should drive a speed
equal to:

◆ Your IQ
◆ Your cat's IQ
◆ Your total cholesterol count
◆ The number of angels that can fit on
the head of a pin
◆ The number of points Michael
Jordan scored in his last game
◆ The average annual rainfall in the
city where you live
◆ The combined ages of your in-laws
◆ The waist size of your new jeans
multiplied by the waist size you
thought you could fit into

Oops! Was That Your Living Room?

If you live in a residential area, you may be aware that the posted speed limit in that area is 25 or 30 MPH. But that's just for sissies and people with all their teeth.

No idiot driver would drive that slow (except on the freeway). Face it, if you're in a residential area, you're probably trying to get away from your family or those people you've been mooching off of for the past six years. Speed is of the essence.

For idiot drivers, the residential

speed limit is however fast you can go without your dog and your kids falling out of the back of the pickup. Well, at least the dog.

Slow Children

Areas near schools often have lower speed limits than nearby streets. This is to protect children as they cross the street to vandalize nearby property.

Idiot drivers know better than to ever approach a school zone. School administrators may still have your permanent record on their computer. The same record that shows that you still owe them forty-seven hundred hours of detention.

If, by some circumstance beyond your control, you *do* find yourself in a school zone:

◆ Put a bag over your head and pray that no one spots you

◆ Turn your baseball cap around, lower your jeans to your hips, and say "Yo" to everyone who passes by

◆ Lie down in the backseat and steer with your feet until you are four blocks away

◆ Cry

Lane? What Lane?

Because they have nothing better to do, the government often sends teams of people out in the middle of rush hour to paint lines on the roads. These lines are supposed to indicate "lanes." Unlike bowling lanes, there are usually no gutters, and they are usually not waxed.

Regular drivers go to a lot of trouble to stay in their own lane (supposedly the one on the right side of the road, unless you're in another country, like Louisiana).

Idiot drivers don't have the time or

the intellectual capacity to tell right from left, so they may drive:

◆ On the other side of the road

◆ On the shoulder

◆ On the thigh

◆ Out on a limb

◆ Into the light

◆ Across the neighbor's lawn (watch out for the pink flamingos)

◆ Through the bank lobby (wave to your teller)

◆ Across the end zone (if there's no penalty flag)

- Between a rock and a hard place

- Where no man has gone before

- Over the river and through the woods

- Across the bridges of Madison County

Safety Rules

If you are at all concerned about safety, your idiot driving privileges have just been revoked. Put this book down and leave the room quickly. Do not come back. We have you on video. And we know where you live.

Okay. Now the rest of you idiot drivers know that safety is not the utmost concern in driving. It's not even in the top ten (which are speed, evasiveness, making other drivers' lives a nightmare, causing major traffic tie-ups, applying makeup, escaping getaways, avoiding work, chatting on the cell phone, property damage, and traumatizing small children and the elderly).

The following idiot driver rules will assure that you never inadvertently drive safely in any situation.

Keep Your Hands to Yourself, Buddy

Safe drivers try to keep both hands on the wheel and both eyes on the road at all times. This can be painful. Idiot drivers, on the other hand (or other hands, if you live close to a nuclear reactor), like to use their hands to do many tasks while driving. Including:

◆ Eating shrimp teriyaki with chopsticks

◆ Putting on panty hose

◆ Juggling chain saws

◆ Performing an emergency appendectomy on yourself

◆ Putting on a puppet show for fifteen screaming kids in the backseat

◆ Sitting in the lotus position

◆ Clipping your toenails

◆ Clipping your dog's toenails

◆ Performing a balance beam routine

◆ Finger painting your windshield

◆ Seeing if the gloves fit

◆ Arm wrestling a member of the World Wrestling Federation

◆ Giving birth

◆ Giving birth to a member of the World Wrestling Federation

Hog the Whole Darn Road

Idiot drivers have one basic philosophy when it comes to sharing the road with other vehicles: Don't! You share the road, you have to acknowledge the existence of someone else. So get your big ugly car and drive right down the center of the road. Drive sideways if you have to. Just get everyone else out of the way as soon as possible.

I See an Intersection in Your Future

Regular drivers always try to scan the entire driving scene at least ten seconds ahead. Idiot drivers try to travel with a psychic who can predict whether there are any traffic problems ahead in the next, say, three, four years. If a psychic is unavailable, try a:

◆ Tarot reader

◆ Chiropractor

◆ Hare Krishna

◆ Seeing Eye dog

◆ An alien

Look Out in the Road, a Head

Fairly frequently, small children may run out into the road with no warning. This is because they haven't yet learned how to spend most of their time dating or downloading your credit card number from the Internet.

Safe drivers often learn that they should always be on the lookout for small children. Idiot drivers, however, should practice looking out for:

◆ Scratch-off lottery tickets

◆ The *Exxon Valdez*

◆ Ectoplasm

◆ Bermuda shorts and white socks

◆ Opera singers

◆ Beached whales

◆ Endangered species

◆ Rain forests

◆ Jerry Springer

◆ The cast of *Married with Children*

Bumper-to-Bumper, Cheek-to-Cheek

You may have heard (or seen on an episode of *CHIPs*) that you should leave one car length between you and the driver in front of you for every 10 MPH you are traveling. Forget it.

The rule for idiots is if you can't read the fine print on the vehicle registration, you're too far behind and the car in front of you may actually win. You should never leave a space between you and the car in front of you that is larger than:

◆ The gap between David Letterman's teeth

◆ The gender gap

◆ A pair of jeans from The Gap

◆ The final frontier

Slow Down, I Think I See Elvis

Safe drivers always slow down before entering a curve. Idiot drivers only slow down before entering:

◆ Graceland

◆ The Boston Marathon

◆ A burrito-eating contest

◆ A roomful of people with big muscles and no teeth

◆ A commitment

◆ A hotel lobby full of Shriners

◆ The Miss Warthog beauty contest

◆ A porta-can

◆ Their spouse in the "My Spouse
Is a Louse" poetry contest

And they don't slow down all that
much. Maybe 1 or 2 MPH. And only
for a nanosecond. Forget we even
brought it up.

You Light Up My Life

If your car comes with headlights,
you may be wondering what they are
for. Simple. Use your headlights when
you want to see where you're going. If
you already know where you're going,
there's no point wasting electricity. In

fact, if you'd rather spend less money, instead of turning your headlights on you may use:

◆ A flashlight

◆ A candle

◆ A candelabra

◆ A pocket lighter

◆ A mirror reflecting the moon

◆ A light beer

Failing to Pass

Passing is one of the most exhila-rating parts of the idiot driving experience. There is nothing like flooring the accelerator, throwing all your passengers into the back window, and leaving another car in your dust. It's even more thrilling if you pass the space shuttle.

The traditional approach to passing is to make sure that there is not a solid yellow stripe on your side of the road and to check for oncoming traffic. But what fun is that?

The rule of idiot passing is that you should never allow other cars in front of you. As a result, you may pass another vehicle under any circumstances, including while:

◆ Passing out

◆ Passing the bar exam

◆ Being circumcised

◆ Being hypnotized

◆ On the Slim-Fast program

◆ Playing Twister

◆ In a twister

◆ Watching the movie *Twister*

◆ Fighting with your sister

◆ Deep-sea diving

Cover Your Rearview

If you were concerned with safety, you'd never hang anything from your rearview mirror that would block your view of the road. Of course, then you'd have no way to decorate, and how would you attract the opposite sex?

The idiot rules for what does and does not belong hanging from the rearview mirror are simple. Almost anything goes, except:

◆ Wet panty hose

◆ A roll of toilet paper

◆ A sauerkraut-fragranced deodorizer

- ◆ Your other car

- ◆ Your other spouse

- ◆ Last night's meat loaf

- ◆ A hornet's nest

- ◆ A vampire bat

- ◆ A baseball bat

- ◆ A fifty-foot garden hose

- ◆ A fifty-foot garden snake

- ◆ A chandelier

- ◆ A hammock

- ◆ A bird feeder

- ◆ The Dream Team

Don't Let Pedestrians Walk All Over You

People who walk are too stupid to drive. And you thought *you* were an idiot! And, not only are they stupid, pedestrians are almost always in your way, hanging out in crosswalks, loitering on sidewalks, standing in their pj's on their porch. . . .

As an idiot driver, the only time you should yield to pedestrians is when:

◆ They're bigger than you

◆ They're bigger than your car

- ◆ They're wearing prison garb

- ◆ They're on a pogo stick

- ◆ They're levitating four inches off the ground

- ◆ They're related to you

- ◆ You really want to know where they got that outfit

Four Wheels Beat Two Wheels Any Day

For some reason, the authorities want drivers to treat bicycles as vehicles. What are they, crazy? Just look at a bicycle. Does it have an engine? Does it have doors? Does it have leftovers from last year's potluck dinner in the trunk? Well, no.

It's obvious, even to the idiot driver, that bicycles are not cars and shouldn't be treated as such. Bicycles should be treated as:

◆ Temporary obstructions

◆ Hood ornaments

◆ Speed bumps

◆ Vermin

Driver Signals and Turns

Many cars, except yours, are equipped with signals. These are lights that allow other drivers to know whether you intend to turn, slow down, make a blindfolded U-turn while playing the banjo, etc.

Here are some rules about the use of signals and turning. We'll probably think of more later. Or we may change these. You never know.

Blinking Idiots

Traditional driver's education classes teach students that they should turn on the blinker one hundred feet before they plan to turn. Idiot drivers don't even know what a blinker is. They think that little stick coming out of the side of the steering wheel is a neat place to hang their wet socks so they can air out.

If you are an idiot driver and your socks are dry, you may want to use your blinker, but only after you have completed a turn. Then it is important that you leave it on until the bulb burns out.

In addition to turns, blinkers are also good for signaling that:

◆ You're thinking about switching political parties

◆ You think the new fall fashions are ugly

◆ Your checking account is overdrawn

◆ You could use an antacid

◆ You have a cramp in your foot

◆ You have to go to the bathroom

◆ Your inner child has to go to the bathroom

◆ Your inner child has already gone to the bathroom

Is That the Signal for Bunt or Pop Fly?

When their blinkers are not working, regular drivers often resort to arm and hand signals. You, the idiot driver, have probably seen a vast repertoire of these signals.

Here is a simple set of signals for idiot drivers to let anyone else who dares to be on the road at the same time know how they're feeling. You may want to write these in waterproof marker on your forehead so you can read them in the rearview mirror in an emergency.

- Left arm straight out window — Moody

- Left arm out window, forearm up — Perky

- Left arm out window, forearm down — Pissed

- Right arm out window — Confused

- Both arms out window — Adventurous

- Both feet out window — Laid back, mellow

- Head out window — Like a dog

- Passenger out window — Happier, now, thank you

Turn Me Over, I Think I'm Done

Most drivers believe they must be in the proper lane to make a turn. Idiot drivers believe they must be in the proper frame of mind to make a turn. Before you turn, always:

◆ Eat a well-balanced breakfast (one serving from the dark chocolate group and two servings from the milk chocolate group)

◆ Make sure you wear comfortable underwear

◆ Get plenty of rest (behind the wheel if necessary)

- Ask your therapist if you're ready

- Consult your horoscope

- Read *I'm Okay, You're Only Mediocre*

- Chant your affirmation ("I am worthy of turning right at this corner. . . .")

Boy, Is My Light Red

It is traditional for drivers to come to a complete stop at a red light. It is also very amusing to watch. If you want to be entertained, just pull up a lawn chair at a stoplight and laugh at all the unnecessary braking and stalling.

It is also true that most cities allow drivers to turn right on red after coming to a complete stop and making sure there is no oncoming traffic. Idiot drivers, on the other hand, may turn right on red if:

◆ It's your birthday

◆ It's payday

◆ The sun's out

◆ There is static on your radio

◆ Red is your favorite color

◆ Red is your dog's favorite color

◆ You're Irish

◆ You're an Irish setter

Offensive Driving

Most drivers practice defensive driving, so, of course, idiot drivers drive offensively. You'll never score if you're always on defense. Anyone who's watched thirty-one Super Bowls could tell you that.

Offensive drivers always:

◆ Enter an intersection two seconds before the light turns green

◆ Never bathe before taking the wheel

◆ Use the sidewalks when the opposition is blocking the road

◆ Drive with their doors open to prevent other drivers from passing

◆ Weave through lanes in a serpentine fashion

◆ Drive at random speeds so the opposition doesn't know what to expect

Space Cushions from Mars

If you wanted to give other drivers a chance to react to your idiotic driving maneuvers, you'd leave what is known in driving terminology as a "space cushion" between your car and the others on the road. But, as we have mentioned earlier, if you are a true idiot driver you have run all the other cars (not to mention pedestrians, bicyclists, trucks, wildlife, and construction crews) off the road. That's plenty of space cushion. In this solar system and beyond.

Driver Beware

Defensive drivers never assume that other drivers will actually obey the law. That is because they have seen the way you drive. Therefore, you may drive however you want. Let the other driver beware.

Idiot drivers never assume:

- The world is round

- The Earth revolves around the Sun

- Shakespeare was English

- The lid's on the salt shaker

We Should Stop Meeting This Way

If you should meet another driver in your lane, the best thing to do is shake hands and exchange business cards. If you don't have a business card, exchange baseball cards.

Communicating with Other Drivers

Typically, regular drivers use their lights, their horn, or their emergency signals to communicate with other drivers. But the idiot driver knows there are so many better ways to let other drivers know what you think, including:

◆ Scorecards like they use at the Olympics

◆ Megaphones

◆ Personal ads

◆ ESP

- ◆ ESPN

- ◆ Two tin cans and a string

- ◆ Poison blow darts

- ◆ Signal fire on the hood

- ◆ Morse code

Accidents Happen

If you do your job, sooner or later you will be involved in an accident. No, we don't mean the kind that involves having to set up a college fund instead of retiring. We mean the vehicular kind.

Your goal in an accident is to try to

make it as much fun as possible. Be forewarned that other drivers and the police will be no help here because for some reason they think accidents are a *big problem*. Tell them to lighten up.

A Bang-Up Job

Most drivers spend all their time and energy trying to avoid a collision, minimize injury, and prevent damage. As a result, they're always having to watch the road, wear their seat belts, and actually keep all four wheels on the ground. Is that the way you want to live? We think not.

Since accidents are unavoidable, the idiot driver puts his or her focus on trying to avoid blame. This can be done by:

◆ Flirting with the other driver so he or she doesn't press charges

◆ Strapping your dog into the driver's seat and claiming he was driving

◆ Getting Scotty to beam you up

◆ Blaming your mother (It helps if you have a note from your therapist saying she or he agrees that everything in your life is your mother's fault.)

◆ Quickly choosing an alias

◆ Claiming diplomatic immunity

◆ Speaking in tongues

The Skid in Me

If the roads are slippery or your tires have no tread (a prerequisite for the idiot driver), you will find yourself occasionally in a skid. When this happens, you should:

◆ Call your Psychic Friend on your cell phone and ask her what to do

◆ Break out the champagne

◆ Close your eyes and repeat, "There's no place like home"

- ◆ Flap your arms

- ◆ Sing the *Wheel of Fortune* theme song

- ◆ Fantasize

- ◆ Think of how you can blame this on your spouse

- ◆ Go, "Wheeee!"

No Returns, No Exchanges

If you get involved in an accident, the other driver may try to get you to write down your name, license number, and insurance company information. Don't do it. These may be held against you in a court of law.

Leigh Anne Jasheway

The only things you should write down when involved in an accident are:

◆ Your measurements

◆ Your favorite color

◆ The words to your favorite commercial jingle

◆ Your shoe size

◆ Your score on the *Glamour* "Rate Your Mate" quiz

◆ Your answer to this question: "If you were a tree, what kind of tree would you be?"

Parking Rules

Park It Here

Believe it or not, there are not only rules for when your car is in motion; the authorities want to tell you what to do when your car is just sitting there minding its own business. Where will it stop? Oh, the injustice of it all.

Here's one of the stupid parking rules. You're not going to believe this. You are not supposed to park in the middle of a tunnel, on a sidewalk, or within fifteen feet of a railroad track! Yeah, right. Where are you supposed to park? One of those spaces with a meter in front of it? Like that's going to happen.

The only places we advise that you not park are:

◆ Within 150 feet of the IRS building

◆ In a pothole

◆ On your spouse

◆ Under a flock of geese

◆ Your mother-in-law's kitchen

◆ Wyoming

All Fired Up and No Place to Park

Supposedly, you shouldn't ever park closer than ten feet from a fire hydrant because a fire truck may need to use the hydrant to put out a fire. Is that your problem? Did you put the fire hydrant in such an inconvenient spot? No, you have better things to spend your time doing.

The only fire hydrant rules that the idiot driver should be aware of are *never*:

◆ Invite a fire hydrant out to dinner

◆ Wear a fire hydrant on a gold chain around your neck

◆ Line dance with a fire hydrant

Roll, Roll, Roll Your Car

If you have to park your vehicle on a hill, you could put on your parking brake to prevent it from rolling down the hill and hitting several other cars and careening through a plate glass window wiping out several cases of deli meats before coming to a stop. Or you could just enjoy the action. Your choice.

Driving Etiquette

In addition to driving for safety, many drivers follow certain etiquette rules.

I Was Here First

An example of these rules is that when two drivers arrive at a stop sign at the same time, the driver on the right is supposed to go through the intersection first.

This may be polite, but it's time-consuming, and it allows another driver to get the jump on you if you're both going to the same big sale down at Wal-Mart (and it doesn't help that the other driver's actually headed in the right direction).

It makes much more sense when two drivers arrive at a stop sign simultaneously that who goes first be decided by any or all of the following methods:

♦ Who has the most expensive car

♦ Who has the best hair

♦ Who can stick their tongue out the farthest

♦ Who remembers all the words to the *Brady Bunch* theme song

♦ Rock, scissors, paper

♦ GRE scores

♦ Hip size

Honk If You're Awake

Somewhere in the middle of your steering wheel is your horn. Try to find it. We'll wait.

Most drivers only use the horn to avoid an accident. That's like having supernatural powers and only using them for good. Idiot drivers honk for all kinds of reasons. Here is a handy reference chart for honking:

◆ One short honk: "Time to wake up, buddy."

◆ One long honk: "I'm single."

◆ Two short honks: "Those are some biceps."

◆ Two long honks: "Can't you see I have screaming children in here?"

◆ Three short honks: "Cool song on the radio, dude."

◆ Three long honks: "Did you know there's an old woman in tennis shoes hanging from your rear bumper?"

You can come up with more of your own. Additionally, you may want to spend a little extra money for a really annoying horn, such as one that plays the "Macarena." This is money well spent.

E.T. Phone Home

If you cared about being nice, you would not use your cellular phone when traffic is heavy. This could cause an accident, or better yet, annoy everyone around you.

The only etiquette rules for cell phone use that apply to idiot drivers are these. Never use a cell phone when:

◆ You don't have one

◆ There's a chance the call will be traced and you will be put in jail

◆ The electromagnetic field causes the metal plate in your head to vibrate

◆ Eight out of ten of your personalities
vote against it

Ms. Manners Slept Here

There are some etiquette rules that
would behoove (you may have to look
that word up) us all to follow. They
are:

◆ When eating in the car, you should
always keep your elbows off the
dashboard.

◆ When making introductions during
a seven-car pileup, it is proper to
introduce drivers in order of respon-
sibility for the wreck. Example:

"Harry, this is Susan. She hit me from behind while applying a third coat of mascara. . . . "

◆ You should always refer to other drivers as "Ma'am" or "Sir" when presenting them with a visual indication of your feeling for their driving skills.

◆ Your radio should never be louder than a sonic boom.

◆ It is impolite to shower while driving.

◆ Never sleep with a traffic officer on the first ticket.

Miscellaneous Idiot Driving Rules

◆ Never yield to anyone. Yielding is a sign of weakness.

◆ Never stop until you see the checkered flag.

◆ The other driver is the enemy. Never do what he or she expects you to do.

◆ You get less tire wear if your car spends more time in the air than on the road.

◆ Those orange cones can be pawned for a quarter each.

◆ If your tires don't screech, you're not trying hard enough.

◆ The person with the rudest bumper sticker gets the parking space.

◆ The proper color for passengers is green, although ashen gray is also acceptable in certain circumstances.

◆ When you hear a siren, turn your radio up louder.

◆ Be proud of your dents.

◆ Don't put on airs. By this we mean, don't sport a PBS bumper sticker or strap a ballet company to the hood of your car.

◆ When entering the freeway, come to a complete stop. Use this time to go over all the new rules of driving you have learned in this book.

Highway Signs and Their Meanings

The Highway Department spends millions of dollars every year putting up signs and signals to help drivers avoid accidents. You'd think with all the money they spend they could at least get some nice colors like mauve or puce, but no, we get the same old signs in the same ugly colors year after year.

It is not at all important for the idiot driver to read or follow highway signs and signals, but it does provide something to do on long drives. So, if you want, here is all the information you need on this subject.

Go Ahead, Red's Not in My Color Chart

Traffic signals usually come with three different colored lights:

◆ A green light means, "Spend a few minutes contemplating the meaning of life and your place in the universe."

◆ A yellow light means, "Speed up or call for pizza on your cell phone."

◆ A red light, "Go, but be sure to wave to the nice people who are honking at you."

We here at Driving for Idiots would like to suggest a few more lights to spice things up:

◆ Blue light: "Special on Aisle 14 on adult diapers"

◆ Purple light: "Cut back on Prozac dosage"

◆ White light: "Say hello to your dead Aunt Edwina"

Sign Me Up Now

There are way too many highway signs for the average idiot driver to commit to memory. We advise you take the following few pages and have them tattooed on your arm.

Stop, unless you stopped last time

Go ahead, stop
at Stuckeys for
a pecan log

Many pretty
colors ahead

Thinner cars
only

Strange-looking
arrows in the
road ahead

Driving
for
Idiots

Church ahead—
have money
ready for offering

Republicans only

People practicing
alternative
lifestyles ahead—
enter at own risk

When you see
someone's head-
lights, turn
around and go
in the other
direction

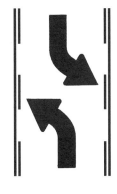

Dating lane

Snakes

Choose another
letter

Beware of
pickpockets

Trucks jacked
up on triangles
ahead

REST AREA
1 MILE

All bath-
rooms are
closed

If you're fed up with not being able to pass anyone on the road, here's your chance

Stick people with large butts in the road

Unless you're really slow, in which case you can't read this sign, and you should drive right down the center stripe

Pedestrians are crossing themselves ahead; go ahead and speed through—if God doesn't protect them, they don't deserve to live

EMERGENCY PARKING ONLY

Park only if your car is on fire, your water just burst, that hangnail started to bleed again, your sister called on the cell phone and needs shoe shopping tips, you glanced in the rearview mirror and noticed your hair looks funky . . .

PASS WITH CARE

Or at least fake it

DEER XING

Deer aren't actually crossing, they're standing on the side of the road looking like they might bolt out at any second so that you drive 40 MPH under the speed limit just in case. This is the way deer entertain themselves since they don't get cable. No, they just don't get it.

No rednecks
next three
miles

Phones stay in
the right lane

Well, there you go. Everything you need to be an idiot driver just like the rest of them.

Gentlemen—and ladies—start your engines.